Little Stars

Little Stars GYMNASTICS

A CRABTREE SEEDLINGS BOOK

Taylor Farley

CRABTREE
PUBLISHING COMPANY
WWW.CRABTREEBOOKS.COM

I love **gymnastics**.

I go to gymnastics class.

We use soft **pads** to stay safe.

We wear **stretchy** clothes.

We stretch, jump, and bend.

Our teacher helps us do **somersaults**.

We do **straddle levers.**

Some of us do the **splits**.

Sometimes we use the rings.

We walk on the balance beam.

Gymnastics makes us strong!

Glossary

gymnastics (jim-NASS-tiks): Gymnastics are difficult and controlled body movements.

pads (PADS): Pads are soft cushions that are used for protection.

somersaults (SUHM-er-sawlts): Somersaults are rolls where the head goes down on the floor and the body rolls forward over the head.

splits (SPLITS): The splits is a move where the body slides to the floor with the legs spread in opposite directions.

straddle lever (STRAD-uhl LEV-ur): A straddle lever is a move where the body is supported with the hands and the legs are off the floor and out to opposite sides.

stretchy (STRECH-ee): Stretchy material can be made wider or longer when pulled.

Index

School-to-Home Support for Caregivers and Teachers

Crabtree Seedlings books help children grow by letting them practice reading. Here are a few guiding questions to help the reader build his or her comprehension skills. Possible answers are included.

Before Reading

- **What do I think this book is about?** I think this book is about gymnastics. It might tell us about different gymnastics moves, like the one on the cover.
- **What do I want to learn about this topic?** I want to learn how children practice gymnastics.

During Reading

- **I wonder why...** I wonder why gymnasts wear stretchy clothes.
- **What have I learned so far?** I learned that children go to gymnastics class. They learn to do somersaults, straddle levers, and splits.

After Reading

- **What details did I learn about this topic?** I learned that gymnasts use soft pads to stay safe. They use rings and balance beams.
- **Write down unfamiliar words and ask questions to help understand their meaning.** I see the word *somersaults* on page 13 and the word *splits* on page 15. The other vocabulary words are listed on pages 22 and 23.

Library and Archives Canada Cataloguing in Publication

Title: Little stars gymnastics / Taylor Farley.
Other titles: Gymnastics
Names: Farley, Taylor, author.
Description: Series statement: Little stars | "A Crabtree seedlings book". | Includes index. |
Previously published in electronic format by Blue Door Education in 2020.
Identifiers: Canadiana 20200378902 | ISBN 9781427129796 (hardcover) | ISBN 9781427129970 (softcover)
Subjects: LCSH: Gymnastics—Juvenile literature.
Classification: LCC GV461.3 .F37 2021 | DDC j796.44—dc23

Library of Congress Cataloging-in-Publication Data

Names: Farley, Taylor, author.
Title: Little stars gymnastics / Taylor Farley.
Other titles: Gymnastics
Description: New York, NY : Crabtree Publishing Company, [2021] | Series: Little stars: a Crabtree seedlings book | Includes index.
Identifiers: LCCN 2020049355 | ISBN 9781427129796 (hardcover) | ISBN 9781427129970 (paperback)
Subjects: LCSH: Gymnastics--Juvenile literature.
Classification: LCC GV461.3 .F37 2021 | DDC 796.44--dc23
LC record available at https://lccn.loc.gov/2020049355

e-book ISBN 978-0-997240-13-9

Print book version produced jointly with Blue Door Education in 2021 Printed in the U.S.A./032022/RR20220126

Photo credits: Cover and page 9 photo: Tatyana Vyc-shutterstock; stars illustration on cover and throughout © Casablanka-shutterstock; pages 3, 4 and 12 © Susan Chiang-istockphoto; page 7 © Valentino Visentini | Dreamstime; pages 10 and 11 © aphichart-istockphoto, KathyDewar-istockphoto, lanych-istpckphoto; page 14 © Sveta Orlova-shutterstock; page 15 © Akvafoto2012 | Dreamstime.com; page 17 © Sergei Kazakov-shutterstock; page 18 © ssj414-istockphoto; page 21 © Julenochek-shutterstock

St. Catharines, Ontario